BEYOND RUBIK'S CUBE

HOW TO INVENT

Lynn Huggins-Cooper

QED Publishing

Created for QED Publishing, Inc. by Tall Tree Ltd
Editors: Emma Marriott and Jon Richards
Designers: Jonathan Vipond
and Malcolm Parchment
Illustrator: Tanja Komadina at Advocate Art
Cover Photography: Michael Wicks

QED Project Editor: Tasha Percy
QED Editorial Director: Victoria Garrard
QED Art Director: Laura Roberts-Jensen
Copyright © QED Publishing 2014

First published in the UK in 2014 by
QED Publishing
A Quarto Group company
The Old Brewery
6 Blundell Street
London, N7 9BH

www.qed-publishing.co.uk

A catalogue record for this book is available
from the British Library.

ISBN 978 1 78171 563 5

Printed and bound in China

Website information is correct at time
of going to press. However, the publishers
cannot accept liability for any information
or links found on third-party websites.

WORDS IN **BOLD** ARE
FOUND IN THE GLOSSARY

CONTENTS

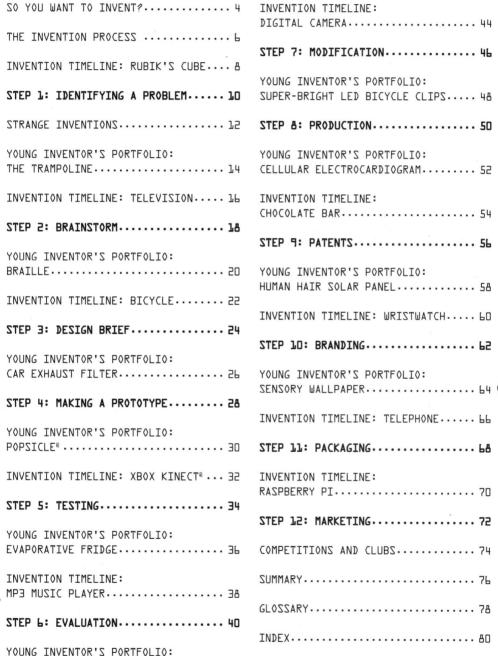

SO YOU WANT TO INVENT?

Look around you, and you can see inventions everywhere. Inventing happens when somebody sees a problem — and invents something to fix it!

What do you think an inventor looks like? Do you think of a whacky-looking man with mad hair and thick glasses? Think again. Inventors are ordinary people just like you.

You have probably invented things already. Have you ever built anything or created your own games? That's inventing.

Have you ever changed something to make it work better? Maybe part of your bike? That's inventing.

Have you ever puzzled over a problem and thought of a way to solve it? That's inventing.

These toy cars have been made out of soft drink cans.

Working out how to fix your bicycle might lead to new ideas.

An old bottle might provide the perfect solution to a problem.

Have you ever used something old and broken to make something new? That's inventing too!

Have you ever thought of a new way to use an object? That's also inventing!

These low-carbon charcoal fuel discs were invented by Kenyan teenagers. They are made from recycled waste.

This book is full of inventors who have created whole new objects, improved existing ones or found new and innovative ways to use old objects and used materials. Can you do the same?

THE INVENTION PROCESS

To be an inventor, you need to follow a process, which is made up of a series of steps. This will take your invention from an idea in your head to an actual product.

» STEP 1

IDENTIFY A PROBLEM OR NEED

» STEP 2

BRAINSTORM IDEAS

Make drawings and notes

» STEP 3

WORK UP A DESIGN BRIEF

Does it work?

» STEP 4

MAKE A PROTOTYPE

» STEP 5

TEST THE ITEM

Could you make it better?

» STEP 6

EVALUATE YOUR DESIGN

» STEP 7

MAKE ANY MODIFICATIONS OR CHANGES

» STEP 8

GO INTO PRODUCTION

Protect it from copycats

» STEP 9

PATENT YOUR INVENTION

» STEP 10

DEVELOP BRANDING

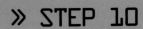

» STEP 11

PACKAGE YOUR PRODUCT

Tell other people

Make your product stand out!

» STEP 12

MARKET YOUR INVENTION

RUBIK'S CUBE

Ernö Rubik invented the Rubik's Cube in 1974 when he was teaching art and **design** in Budapest, Hungary. He liked to invent puzzles to help his students think about 3D shapes. He created a wooden model of his puzzle and everyone was fascinated by the way it moved.

Ernö Rubik
1944–present

The cube is made up of 26 movable blocks. Each side has nine squares, and there are 54 coloured block faces in total.

1974

First wooden model of the Rubik's Cube created.

1975

The cube is mass produced.

1977

The cube appears in stores in Budapest, Hungary. It is initially called the Magic Cube.

1980

Rubik's Cube is made Toy of the Year.

To start with each side of the cube has one colour. Twisting the cube mixes up the colours. There are more than 43 quintillion possible moves, but only one correct solution!

In 1975, a Hungarian toy manufacturer started producing the cubes, and they appeared in the shops in 1977. In 1979, the Rubik's Cube became available around the world. More than 350 million cubes have since been sold.

Rubik's Twist

Rubik's Revenge

» OTHER GAMES

After the success of the original cube, other puzzles were released, including a cube with more pieces called Rubik's Revenge, Rubik's 360 puzzle, Rubik's Twist and Rubik's TouchCube, a touch-sensitive version with no moving parts.

Rubik's 360

Rubik's TouchCube

1981

1999

2014

You Can Do The Cube, a book telling people how to solve the puzzle, is released and sells 1.5 million copies.

Rubik's Cube celebrates its 25th anniversary.

Beyond the Rubik's Cube Exhibition opens.

Ernö Rubik

» STEP 1

IDENTIFYING A PROBLEM

Inventions are created to solve problems or needs. Identifying a need is the first step in the invention process.

Ernö Rubik was a sculptor and architect teaching at a university in Budapest, Hungary. He needed to teach his students how to tackle three-dimensional (3D) problems and wanted to use something that was fun and educational. To do this, he began designing puzzles for them to solve.

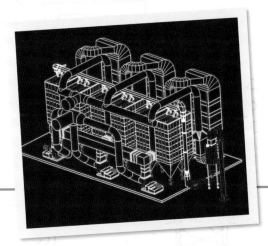

Today, architects use computers to make 3D images of their buildings that they can rotate. Rubik did not have access to modern computers. He made models to help his students think about space and the geometry of three dimensions.

In 1974, when he was 29, Rubik created a cube-shaped puzzle for his students – the first Rubik's Cube. Each side of the cube was made of coloured squares, which the player could move to solve the puzzle.

Robots can be programmed to solve a Rubik's Cube by following a set of mathematical rules.

In order to solve the cube (and make sure that each side only had one colour), the students had to be aware of how moves affected all sides of the 3D puzzle.

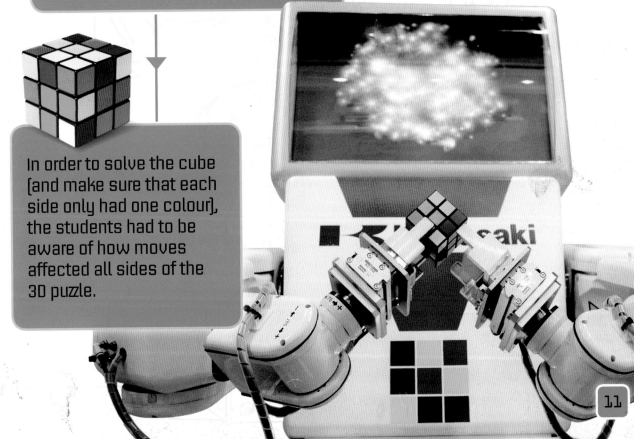

STRANGE INVENTIONS

Inventions are often created to solve problems. New objects are being invented every day – some useful and others just plain weird! The ones that don't become popular often fail to solve a problem – or there is already a better solution!

INVENTION: Dogbrella

Have you ever walked a dog in the rain? They get awfully wet. Enter the Dogbrella. It's basically an upside-down umbrella that shelters your dog! Most people just rub their dog with a towel afterwards, however.

this is really not cool!

INVENTION: Pizza Scissors

Cutting pizza can be tricky, with all the stringy cheese. There are pizza wheels, but they can run away with you and be quite dangerous – so how about a pair of pizza scissors? Or you could just use an old-fashioned knife.

INVENTION:
Atomic Car

In 1958, the Ford Nucleon was invented. It was to be a nuclear-powered car, running for 8000 kilometres without refuelling. There was only one problem — a car carrying a nuclear reactor could cause a huge explosion if it was involved in a crash! The cars were never made.

INVENTION:
Smell-O-Vision

Smell-O-Vision piped scents into the cinema to make a film more realistic. Thirty different smells, including tobacco and garlic, would be pumped into cinemas through tubes beneath the seats. It was only used once in 1960, and audiences did not like the smells, or the hissing coming from under their seats.

YOUNG INVENTOR'S PORTFOLIO

George Nissen was a keen gymnast. He had seen circus acts where trapeze artists used their safety nets to bounce and perform tricks. He wanted to create something to help him train, and to do several tricks in a row.

NAME: George Nissen

AGE: 16

INVENTION: The trampoline

YEAR: 1934

HUH!

WHAT?

BOING!

More than 25 years after developing the trampoline, George showed off his invention with the help of 'Victoria', a kangaroo.

In 1934, George and his coach built the first prototype, out of an iron frame, a piece of canvas and some rubber springs. He carried on refining his invention to improve it.

George called his invention the trampoline after the Spanish word *trampolin*, which means 'diving board'.

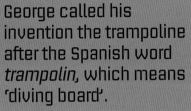

In 1956, George set up a factory in Essex, UK, and made trampolines there for many years. In 2000, trampolining was included as an event in the Olympic Games. Not bad for an invention created by a 16-year-old!

BOING!

» SPACEBALL

George Nissen also invented a game called Spaceball. Two players on each team try to score points by throwing a ball through a hoop — while they are bouncing on trampolines!

TELEVISION

Television wasn't invented by one person — but British scientist John Logie Baird was the first to give a public demonstration of television to the world.

Baird used spinning discs to create television pictures. He scanned images with a spinning disc full of tiny holes. Light came through the holes in flashes.

John Logie Baird
1888–1946

Baird used junk to create the first television apparatus – boxes, sewing needles, card, the motor from a fan and a biscuit tin. That makes his invention even more amazing!

1884

1924

1926

Paul Nipkow
1860–1940

German scientist Paul Nipkow sends images over wires using his invention, the 'electric telescope'.

John Logie Baird builds a television and transmits some flickering images across a room.

Baird demonstrates his television at the Royal Institution in London.

Baird converted the flashes into electrical signals. He sent the signals and these made a fuzzy picture – the world's first television transmission.

Baird demonstrates an early television set in 1929

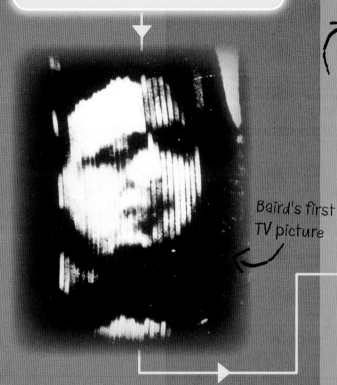

Baird's first TV picture

He demonstrated his television to scientists at the Royal Institution in London. In 1927, he sent pictures from London to Glasgow, and in 1928 he sent the first pictures from Britain to America.

1928

1940

1946

1962

Baird sends TV pictures from Britain to America.

Peter Goldmark develops the first commercial colour television. It produces coloured pictures with the use of a spinning three-coloured disk.

RCA Model 630-TS becomes the first mass-produced TV set.

First satellite TV signal relayed from Europe to North America.

BLEEP BLEEP

17

BRAINSTORM

Brainstorming is a thinking session with the focus on producing ideas. Inventors use brainstorming to come up with new ideas or develop existing ones at the beginning of a project. It can also help inventors come up with answers to tricky problems.

Be very clear about the problem you want to solve before you start. This will help you to focus.

When you are brainstorming, write down any thoughts and ideas you have about your project — even if they are completely random. Include ideas about the shape and size of your invention, and how it will work.

Include *everything*. However silly or obvious an idea may seem, make sure you include it. It might spark new ideas later in the process.

Share ideas with others. It's a good idea to bounce thoughts around. Allow people to add their own thoughts to ideas that have already been written down.

Brainstorming is about getting everything out into the open in a safe space, without anything being criticised or praised. Make sure that everyone in the group gets a chance to contribute.

After the brainstorming, have another group discussion to develop and build on the ideas. It helps to have someone act as a facilitator — their job is to make sure everyone is heard and all the ideas are recorded.

YOUNG INVENTOR'S PORTFOLIO

Have you heard of Braille? It is a system to help blind people to read, using a pattern of raised dots that they can feel with their fingertips.

Can you tell what word this person is reading?

NAME: Louis Braille

AGE: 15

INVENTION: Braille

YEAR: 1824

Louis Braille
1809–1852

Louis Braille was blinded in an accident when he was 3 years old. He went to a special school for blind people, but found it frustrating that he could not read books and discover things easily for himself.

The alphabet chart for English language Braille

A	B	C	D	E	F	G	H	I
●○	●○	●●	●●	●○	●●	●●	●○	○●
○○	●○	○○	○●	○●	●○	●●	●●	●○
○○	○○	○○	○○	○○	○○	○○	○○	○○

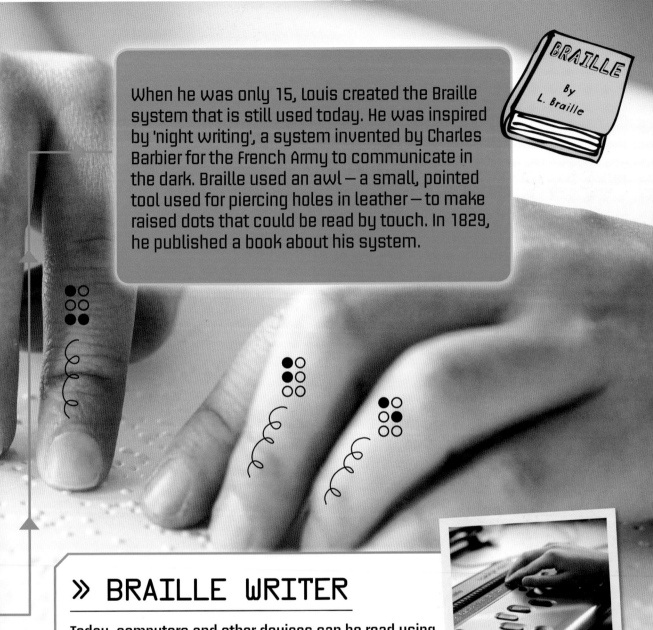

When he was only 15, Louis created the Braille system that is still used today. He was inspired by 'night writing', a system invented by Charles Barbier for the French Army to communicate in the dark. Braille used an awl — a small, pointed tool used for piercing holes in leather — to make raised dots that could be read by touch. In 1829, he published a book about his system.

BRAILLE
By
L. Braille

» BRAILLE WRITER

Today, computers and other devices can be read using Braille and there are computer printers that **emboss** Braille. It can also be typed using a special typewriter which uses combinations of keys to produce letters, rather than a single key for each letter. The Braille letters are then punched into a piece of paper.

Braille typewriter

J K L M N O P Q R S T U V W X Y Z

INVENTION TIMELINE

BICYCLE

Bicycles were introduced in the 1800s, and there are now more than a billion of them around the world. The first bicycle was known as a 'dandy horse' — it was an odd contraption that the rider had to push along with his or her feet.

The penny-farthing was named after two coins – the large penny and the small farthing.

By the 1860s, bone shaking machines such as the penny-farthing were rattling about the streets. They made for an uncomfortable ride!

1817

1860s

1885

The dandy horse is invented.

A French inventor, probably Ernest Michaux, adds the first pedals to a bicycle.

Invention of the safety bicycle.

John Kemp Starley 1854 –1901

In 1885, John Kemp Starley invented the 'safety bicycle'. It had two similar-sized wheels, driven by a chain, and a hollow steel frame, which made the bicycle lighter. Crucially, it also had a steerable front wheel – which earlier bicycles did not have!

The 'safety bicycle'

John Dunlop
1840–1921

Modern racing bikes have light frames made of carbon fibre.

Bicycle rides became even more comfortable in 1888 when John Dunlop introduced the pneumatic tyre, which was cushioned with air.

1888

1960s

1996

Pneumatic tyres are invented.

Light racing bicycles with dropped handlebars become popular.

Mountain biking introduced as an Olympic sport.

DESIGN BRIEF

Once you have worked out what your invention needs to do, it's time to get a design down on paper. It needs to grab people's attention, so appearance can be important, but it still needs to work correctly. To do this, you'll need to create a design **brief**. This is a written document which tells other people how you want your invention to look and function.

Identify the aim of your invention. Make sure you know exactly what the invention needs to do for the finished design to be successful.

Create a design brief. This helps you to organise your ideas in one place. So try and make sure that all the issues you might face when you are making your invention prototype have been thought about.

Make sure you choose the right materials for the job — what qualities do they have that might make them a good choice?

Who is your target audience and who will use your invention? Do they have particular needs that should be considered?

Think about how you want your invention to look. Make rough sketches with notes — they don't have to be perfect!

Keep returning to your brief and use it for reference to guide your work.

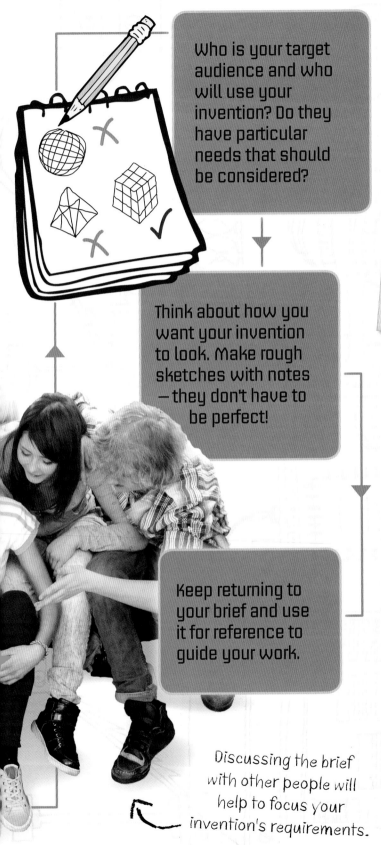

Discussing the brief with other people will help to focus your invention's requirements.

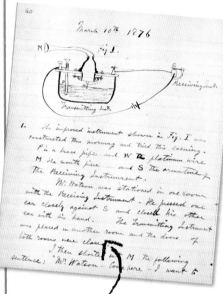

These drawings made by Alexander Graham Bell show his thought processes behind inventing the telephone.

» MAKE NOTES

Keep records of your designs. Daniel Drawhaugh wished he had! He claimed to have invented the telephone before Alexander Graham Bell. However, he had no record of his design, so the Supreme Court rejected his claim. Bell had excellent records and was awarded the **patent** — and his place in history!

YOUNG INVENTOR'S PORTFOLIO

Param Jaggi's invention could help save the environment! The young American invented a clever device that turns the carbon dioxide produced by cars into oxygen.

NAME: Param Jaggi

AGE: 17

INVENTION:
Car exhaust filter

YEAR: 2011

O_2

Algae

Param first noticed a problem when he started learning to drive. Cars release lots of harmful gases into the air, and this damages the environment. He decided to solve this issue by removing the nasty gases.

His invention uses **algae** as a filter. The device plugs into the exhaust pipe of a car and the algae inside change the gases coming out of the car into clean oxygen. Each device costs around £20.

O_2

PARAM 1

Yuck!

Vrooooom!

Yuck!

Param's algae-packed invention.

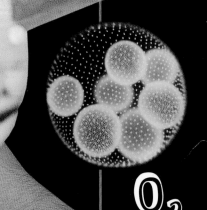

O_2

Param's system, which has now been patented, won an Environment Protection Agency sustainability award in 2011. In the same year, Param won a scholarship to college. He is now working on refining his invention.

O_2

OTHER USES

Param's invention might be used for more than car emissions — it could possibly be used in power stations to stop pollution entering the air, and even improve the environment!

MAKING A PROTOTYPE

A **prototype** is the first actual version of an invention. Creating a prototype helps inventors see if their ideas actually work, and enables them to make changes before going into production. The prototype of the Rubik's Cube was made from wood!

The wooden prototype of the Rubik's Cube.

Create a non-working model of your design. This is a quick way of seeing how your invention will look.

WHIRR

CLICK!

The latest 3D printing technology can create a fully working prototype cheaply and easily. It can be used to iron out flaws in a design, and avoid costly mistakes.

3D printers can create a cheap working prototype.

>Print

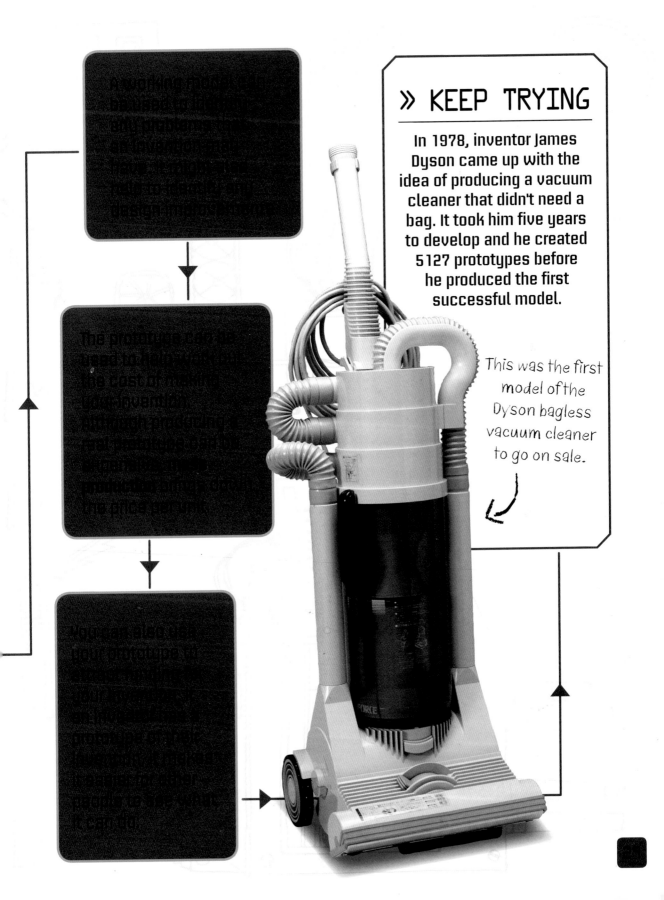

» KEEP TRYING

In 1978, inventor James Dyson came up with the idea of producing a vacuum cleaner that didn't need a bag. It took him five years to develop and he created 5127 prototypes before he produced the first successful model.

This was the first model of the Dyson bagless vacuum cleaner to go on sale.

YOUNG INVENTOR'S PORTFOLIO

In 1905, 11-year-old Frank Epperson accidentally invented one of the most popular Summer treats. One cold night, he left a drink outside, with a stirring stick still in it. The next morning, Frank discovered that his drink had frozen with the stick inside — and made a lolly!

NAME: Frank Epperson

AGE: 11

INVENTION: Popsicle®

YEAR: 1905

Frank and his granddaughter enjoy a Popsicle in this photo taken in 1973 to celebrate the 50th anniversary of applying for the patent.

Yippee!

Yummy!

In 1923, 18 years after he first invented the frozen treat, Frank applied for a patent for it. His invention was initially sold as the 'Epsicle Ice Pop', but later became the 'Popsicle'.

The Popsicle Company still exists today and sells more than two billion ice lollies a year! The most popular Popsicle flavour is cherry.

Advertisements, such as this poster from the 1950s, helped to make Popsicles even more popular.

» MONSTER LOLLY

In 2005, the Snapple company attempted to make the world's largest ice lolly. The previous record had been set by a 6.4-metre monster in Holland in 1997. Snapple tried to make a 7.6-metre lolly in New York — but it melted too fast and firefighters had to be called in to hose away kiwi-strawberry sludge!

XBOX KINECT®

Sensors can recognize faces and voices.

Released in 2010 by Microsoft, the Xbox Kinect uses facial, voice and gesture recognition to make players feel like they are part of a video game! People have also started using Kinect in more important ways — such as saving lives!

Moving around controls on-screen characters.

The Kinect uses 3D cameras, microphones and laser sensors to detect your movements. It then makes the character move the same way.

1972	1977	1978	1988

Atari launches Pong, the first commercially successful video game.

Atari releases the Atari 2600, one of the most successful video game consoles ever.

Space Invaders released.

Sega releases the Mega Drive video game console.

The Kinect can be hooked up to an MRI scanner, then controlled by hand and voice commands. This allows doctors to see pictures to guide their work without touching a keyboard and risking contamination.

It can also be used for keyhole surgery, where it controls the movement of robotic instruments inside the body.

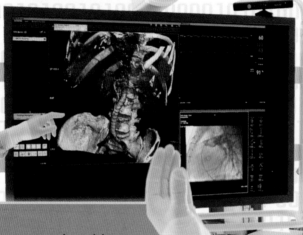

Surgeons using Kinect to perform an operation.

One day, surgeons may be able to use Kinect technology to perform surgery remotely, operating on people in hard-to-reach places such as disaster zones and battlefields.

1994

Sony releases the PlayStation.

2001

Microsoft releases the original Xbox.

2010

Kinect is released.

2013

Microsoft releases the Xbox One with Kinect sensor.

» STEP 5
TESTING

Testing whether an invention works is vital – if it does not function properly, or is not safe then it's back to the drawing board. It is important to check that a product is easy and safe to use before it goes into mass production.

When you test your prototype, think about how it will work in real life, in a variety of different situations. Sometimes, products in development are shown to groups of people as market research, to see what they think.

Use the results of your test to refine and change your invention before it goes into production. This saves time and money later on, and helps to make an invention more successful.

When testing cars, engineers use special dummies which copy how people move in a crash.

Use a 'field test' to test your invention in the place and situation where it will be used. While a field test cannot hope to find all of the strengths and weaknesses of a design, it can help you to think creatively to improve your work.

Thomas Edison
1847–1931

» LIGHT BULB

When trying to invent the light bulb, Thomas Edison tested more than 1600 materials before he found the one that worked. These materials included fishing line, coconut fibres and the hair from a colleague's beard. His notes on the testing filled more than 40,000 pages! In 1879, he found that carbonized bamboo kept the bulb lit for more than 40 hours.

These toys are being tested inside a laboratory to make sure they are safe.

Testing an invention for safety is crucial. If an invention is not safe to use, it cannot be sold. Testing helps to make any safety problems obvious and can stop something that is not safe from going onto the market.

YOUNG INVENTOR'S PORTFOLIO

Emily Cummins started inventing things when she was four years old. She used to make toys out of scraps with her granddad in his garden shed. Today, she still makes things – but these inventions could change the world!

NAME: Emily Cummins

AGE: 18

INVENTION: Evaporative fridge

YEAR: 2005

Emily holding her evaporative fridge in her grandfather's shed, where she has created most of her inventions.

In 2006, Emily entered one of her inventions into a sustainable design competition – a pullable water carrier for use in developing countries. Her device won her a Technology Woman of the Future award.

She has also developed a type of fridge powered by dirty water! It works by **evaporation**, and can be used to keep medicines and food cool. The fridge runs without electricity and can be built using barrels, car parts and easy-to-find materials.

Solar panels provide electricity in sunny, remote areas, such as this hut in the Sahara.

» REMOTE POWER

Getting electricity to homes requires a lot of equipment — including generators, pylons and cables. Some countries can't afford to build the equipment needed to get electricity everywhere, so remote places need to come up with their own, local sources.

This radio is powered by clockwork. Turning the handle charges up a battery.

Emily worked on her plan during a gap year in Namibia, Africa, and gave out the plans for it in townships across southern Africa so people could build their own.

MP3 MUSIC PLAYER

An MP3 media player is a digital audio player that stores and plays MP3 files and other media. MP3 files take up less storage memory than previous files, so you can fit more onto a music player. MP3 players, such as iPods, can store thousands of tunes on one tiny machine!

Karlheinz Brandenburg
1954–present

US inventor Thomas Edison's phonograph recorded sounds on a metal cylinder.

Karlheinz Brandenburg is a German scientist and mathematician who began developing the files that would become MP3s in 1977. He had already developed two earlier versions — the MP1 and the MP2. In 1996, he created the greatly improved MP3 and patented the idea.

1877
Thomas Edison invents the phonograph to create sound recordings.

1889
Emile Berliner starts selling flat discs and players called gramophones.

1982
Compact discs (CDs) are launched.

Brandenburg also developed an MP3 player, but it was not very reliable. In 1997, Tomislav Uzelac of Advanced Media Products created the AMP MP3 Playback Engine, one of the first reliable MP3 players.

Apple's iPod is the world's most popular MP3 player.

Portable MP3 players began to appear in 1999, but they were quite heavy and bulky. Apple introduced iPod MP3 players in 2001, eight months after they released the software iTunes. People use iTunes to buy MP3 versions of music and load the files directly onto their iPod.

1996
MP3s patented.

2001
Apple iPod introduced.

2003
iTunes Music Store launched.

2012
350 millionth iPod sold.

EVALUATION

Evaluation is an important part of any project — especially creating a new invention! It is important to think carefully about how the invention works, and whether it needs changes. Evaluation can identify and look at any problems that have arisen during the testing process.

Does the invention actually work? Can it be used in the way that was intended when it was designed? If not, changes may need to be made.

This car is being tested to make sure that it performs well and is safe.

02
K30

Is the invention made as simply as possible – or has it been over-complicated? Are there things that can be left out or modified?

Is the invention safe as it is, or are changes needed?

Is the idea really new? Are there other very similar products available? Even if there are, the new invention may be a better solution to the problem.

Will the invention cost too much to produce or make in bulk?

Will the invention work well and last – or will it break?

Will people want to use the invention? If so – why?

» WARNING!

Proper evaluation of a product is essential – miss this out and it could fail spectacularly! The Segway, for example – a kind of motorized step or scooter – worked well, and had a lot of publicity, but it failed to sell well and lost lots of money. Its inventors hadn't properly evaluated the product's function and usefulness in everyday life.

The Segway worked well but problems over where to ride, park and charge it led to its failure.

YOUNG INVENTOR'S PORTFOLIO

While working in a factory, a girl called Margaret Knight saw a horrible accident. A steel-tipped shuttle flew out of a weaving loom, hitting and injuring one of her friends.

NAME: Margaret Knight

AGE: 12

INVENTION: Shuttle restraining device

YEAR: 1850

In the 1800s, children often worked in factories to help their families earn a living. Accidents were common and many children were hurt.

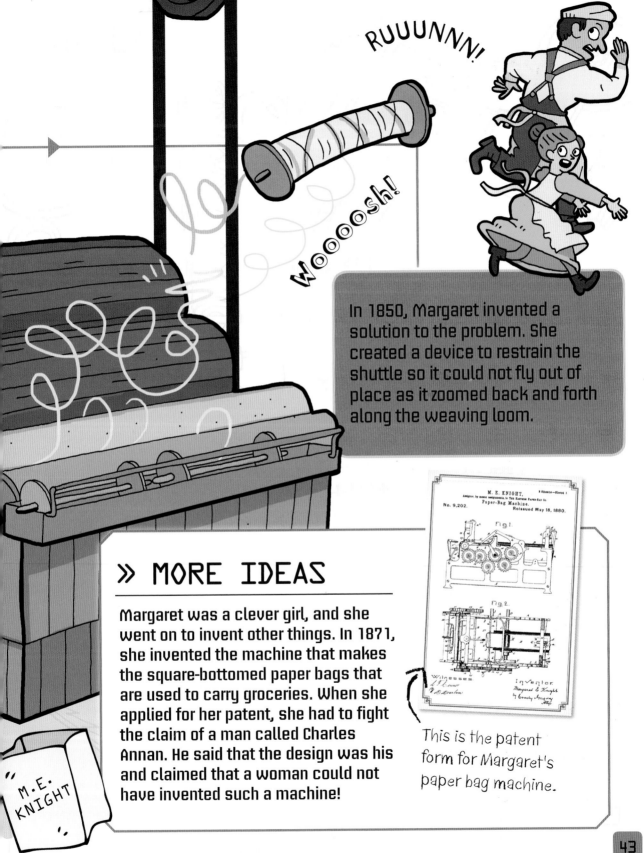

RUUUNNN!

Woooosh!

In 1850, Margaret invented a solution to the problem. She created a device to restrain the shuttle so it could not fly out of place as it zoomed back and forth along the weaving loom.

» MORE IDEAS

Margaret was a clever girl, and she went on to invent other things. In 1871, she invented the machine that makes the square-bottomed paper bags that are used to carry groceries. When she applied for her patent, she had to fight the claim of a man called Charles Annan. He said that the design was his and claimed that a woman could not have invented such a machine!

This is the patent form for Margaret's paper bag machine.

"M.E. KNIGHT"

DIGITAL CAMERA

Cameras have been around in different forms since the first successful photograph was taken around 1826–7 by French inventor Nicéphore Niépce. By 1900, photography had become very popular. The recent invention of digital cameras allows us to take and share photos in an instant.

Steve Sasson
1950–present

Memory card

Unlike old cameras, digital cameras do not need film. They save images electronically on memory cards.

The first digital camera was built in 1975 by the engineer Steve Sasson, who worked for US manufacturer Kodak. It weighed 3.6 kg and recorded black and white images onto a cassette tape. It was not put on sale as the images were very low resolution.

1826-7 1883-9 1900

First successful photograph taken by Niépce of the view from his window.

George Eastman develops photographic film to replace large plates.

Box Brownie camera released.

In 1989, the first digital camera went on sale in Japan. It used an internal memory card to store images. The following year, digital cameras went on sale in the US — but they cost nearly $1000!

Today, inexpensive digital cameras are available and most mobile phones now have them too!

1948   1975   2000   2013

Polaroid release the first instant camera.

First digital camera is built.

First mobile phone with a camera released.

Nokia releases a phone with a 41-megapixel camera.

MODIFICATION

When you 'modify' something, you change it. Making a **modification** to an invention means changing it to make it better or more effective. Sometimes inventions are modified after they have been tested; others are modified after they are on the market, when somebody thinks of an improvement.

The original Cube (above) was modified (below) to meet western safety standards.

Inventors consider a range of questions after they have tested and evaluated their invention. Could it be improved by using a different material?

A technician testing a toy robot.

Hmmmmm?

Could the invention be adapted so it fits its purpose better?

Is the shape right? Does it need to be more streamlined so it can move quicker, or do the edges need to be rounded for safety reasons?

Could the invention be used in different ways, or for different purposes? Sometimes this is only discovered after testing when the inventor is thinking about his or her findings.

Would the invention work better if it was made to a different scale, either smaller or bigger than the prototype?

» CORNFLAKES

Cornflakes were invented by accident while Keith Kellogg and his brother were researching healthy hospital meals. Having left some bread dough to sit for hours, Keith discovered the wheat in it had turned flaky. He toasted the flakes, and found the patients loved them. He then modified his invention, using corn instead of wheat. He launched his company in 1906 — and this later became known as Kellogg's.

Are similar inventions available? If market research shows there are, inventors should be prepared to make changes to ensure they offer an improved version — it doesn't mean an invention has failed.

YOUNG INVENTOR'S PORTFOLIO

Have you ever cycled when it is dark? It is important that you can be easily seen, to avoid having an accident. That is why cyclists wear clothing with reflective strips, and have lights on their bicycles.

NAME: Adam Kassell

AGE: 14

INVENTION: Super-Bright LED Bicycle Clips

YEAR: 2012

Fourteen-year-old Adam Kassell, from Worthing in West Sussex in the UK, went one step further to ensure cycling safety. In 2012, he designed super-bright **LED** bicycle clips that are clipped around the ankles and can be programmed to spell out words! These lights make cyclists more visible to motorists, making cycling in the dark much safer.

Bike lights and reflective strips on clothing are essential kit for cyclists.

In 2012, Adam was one of two winners of the 'We Made It!' competition, which was set up to encourage young inventors in the UK. Prototypes of the winning ideas are created and tested. The aim of the annual competition is to encourage teenagers to think about careers in manufacturing.

Adam and the design for his bicycle clips (below) beat off more than 350 entries to win the competition.

PRODUCTION

Production means making copies of something so that they are ready to sell. The prototype of the Rubik's Cube was made by hand, but the real cubes are made in factories. These steps explain the different parts of production for a Rubik's Cube — the process differs for other products.

A car production assembly line.

Plastic pellets

A Rubik's Cube is made from plastic pellets. These are melted and the molten plastic is injected into a mould.

Two parts of the mould are brought together to create a cavity in the shape of a part of the Rubik's Cube. It could be an edge, a corner or a centre piece.

Cube pieces

The plastic cools in the mould, and it goes hard. When the mould is opened, the cube pieces are removed and the process starts again.

The completed parts are dropped in containers and inspected to make sure they are not faulty or damaged.

All steps in any production process involve checks to see if everything is going well.

» INSPECTION

Checking a Rubik's Cube involves a lot more than just looking at each piece. The thickness, length and width of each piece are checked with a caliper, a micrometer and even a microscope!

A caliper gives accurate measurements.

The pieces are taken to the assembly line. They are put together to make a cube. The centre parts are fixed to the nylon core.

Coloured labels are added to the cube. These are laminated with a special covering to protect them and stop them from peeling off.

YOUNG INVENTOR'S PORTFOLIO

Catherine Wong invented a health test that could save the lives of millions of people, and all while she was still at school! This 16-year-old invented a tiny device that can be connected to a mobile phone to show a person's heartbeat on its screen.

NAME: Catherine Wong

AGE: 16

INVENTION:
Cellular electrocardiogram
(mobile phone heart test)

YEAR: 2012

THUMP!

THUMP!

This patient is attached to an ECG machine.

Catherine's device works like a portable electrocardiogram. Also called an ECG or EKG, these often large pieces of equipment are used at a hospital or doctor's surgery to measure how the patient's heart is beating.

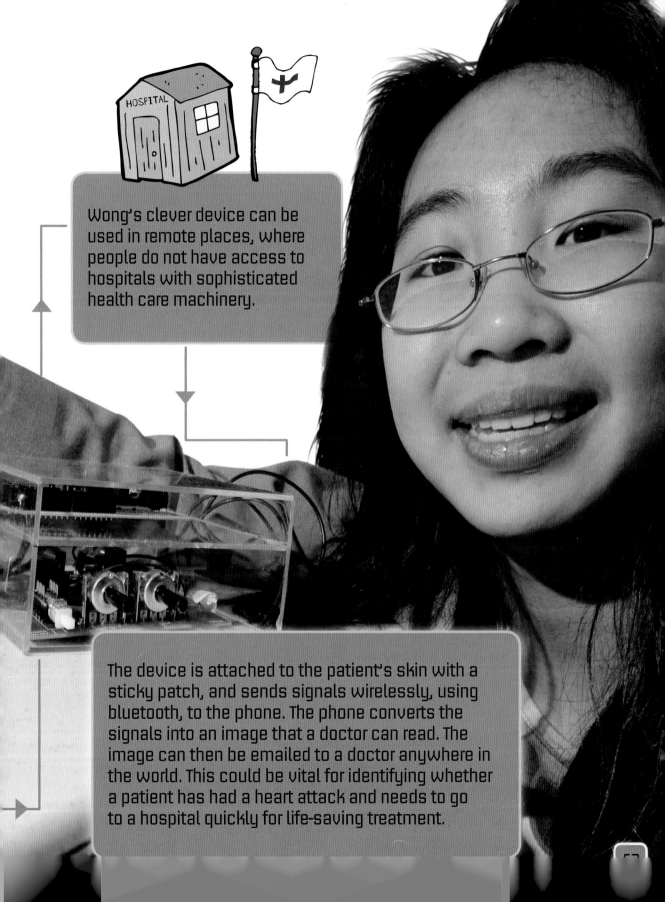

Wong's clever device can be used in remote places, where people do not have access to hospitals with sophisticated health care machinery.

The device is attached to the patient's skin with a sticky patch, and sends signals wirelessly, using bluetooth, to the phone. The phone converts the signals into an image that a doctor can read. The image can then be emailed to a doctor anywhere in the world. This could be vital for identifying whether a patient has had a heart attack and needs to go to a hospital quickly for life-saving treatment.

HOSPITAL

CHOCOLATE BAR

Chocolate is made from roasted cocoa beans. In the Aztec and Mayan cultures of North and Central America, a chocolate drink was used in religious ceremonies. In Europe, chocolate was sweetened by adding sugar and milk. It was first made into bars in the 19th century.

The Mayans drank chocolate with added corn or chilli.

Founded in 1761, Joseph Fry and Sons started out making chocolate tablets for drinking chocolate. In 1847, the company created the first chocolate bar.

1502

Chocolate is brought to Europe from the Americas by Christopher Columbus.

Christopher Columbus 1451–1506

1650

Chocolate becomes a popular drink in Europe.

1847

Joseph Fry and Son create the first chocolate bar.

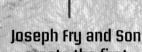

Fry's chocolate bars were made in factories.

The firm first produced Fry's Chocolate Cream Bar in 1866, and it is still in production today. They went on to make over 220 products in the next decade, including the first chocolate Easter egg in 1873.

Keen to try new things, Joseph Fry's grandson discovered how to mix cocoa powder, extracted cocoa butter and sugar to create solid chocolate that was smoother than the chocolate tablets. The result could be moulded into bars and eaten.

Fry poured chocolate over fruit-flavoured creamy centres.

FRY'S CHOCOLATE CREAM

J.S. FRY & SONS, Ltd., MAKERS OF PURE CONCENTRATED

1875

Swiss chocolatier Daniel Peter creates the first milk chocolate bar.

1919

The chocolate companies Cadbury and Fry and Sons merge.

2009

FAIRTRADE

Cadbury's Dairy Milk becomes Fairtrade, raising the living standards of cocoa farmers in Ghana.

PATENTS

Did you know that ideas and inventions can be stolen? But they can also be protected. Governments around the world issue patents to stop people from copying ideas. A patent gives inventors control over the way their inventions are made, used or sold.

This is the 1983 US patent for the Rubik's Cube. The cube was first patented in Hungary and trademarked as 'The Magic Cube'. This changed to the 'Rubik's Cube' for international markets.

A new idea – such as an invention – is called 'intellectual property', and it can be protected by applying for a patent.

A patent is a document that says that the registered inventor has the right to stop other people from copying their idea. Nobody else can make, sell or use another person's patented invention without permission.

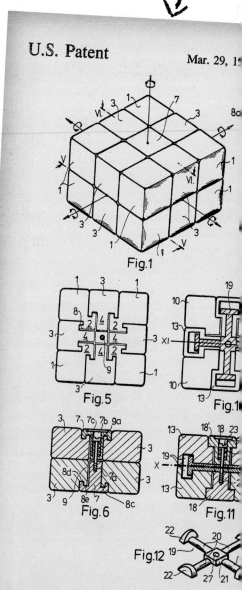

U.S. Patent   Mar. 29, 1

Fig.1

Fig.5   Fig.10

Fig.6   Fig.11

Fig.12

Did you know there are no age restrictions on applying for a patent? The youngest person to be awarded a patent was a four-year-old girl from Texas, who invented an aid for grasping round knobs on drawers and doors.

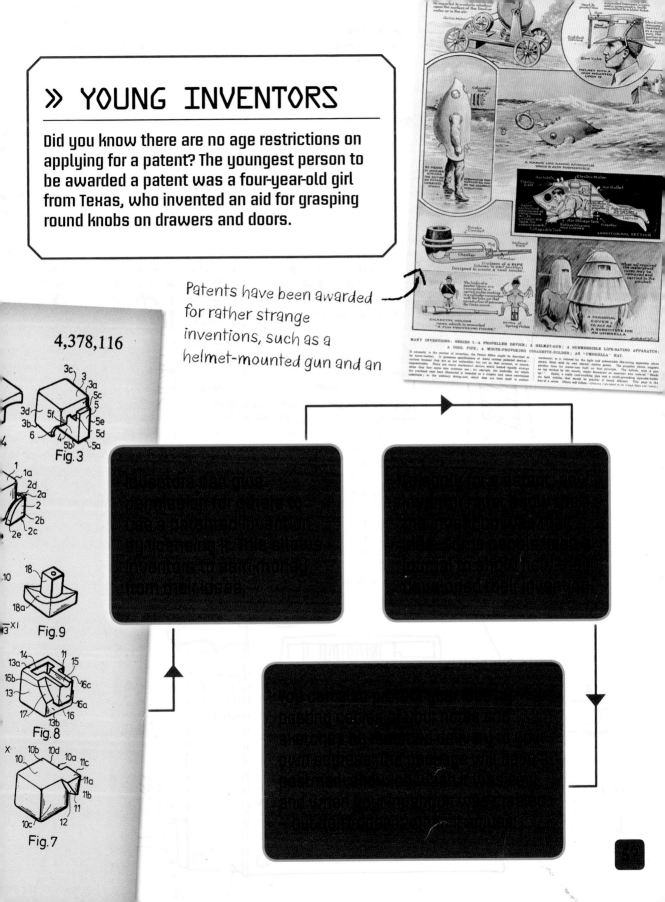

Patents have been awarded for rather strange inventions, such as a helmet-mounted gun and an

4,378,116

3c 3 3a
3d 5c
5f 5e
3b 5d
6 5b 5a
Fig. 3

1 1a
2d
2a
2
2b
2e 2c

10 18
18a
X1
Fig. 9

14 11 15
13a
16b 16c
13 16a
17 16
13b
Fig. 8

X 10b 10d 10a 11c
10 11a
11b
11
10c 12
Fig. 7

YOUNG INVENTOR'S PORTFOLIO

Milan's solar panel can power a light or charge a mobile phone using hair!

NAME: Milan Karki

AGE: 18

INVENTION:
Human hair solar panel

YEAR: 2009

Imagine growing up in a world without electricity. No lights at the touch of a switch, no computers and no TV. Milan Karki grew up in a remote area of Nepal in a small village that was not connected to the electricity grid.

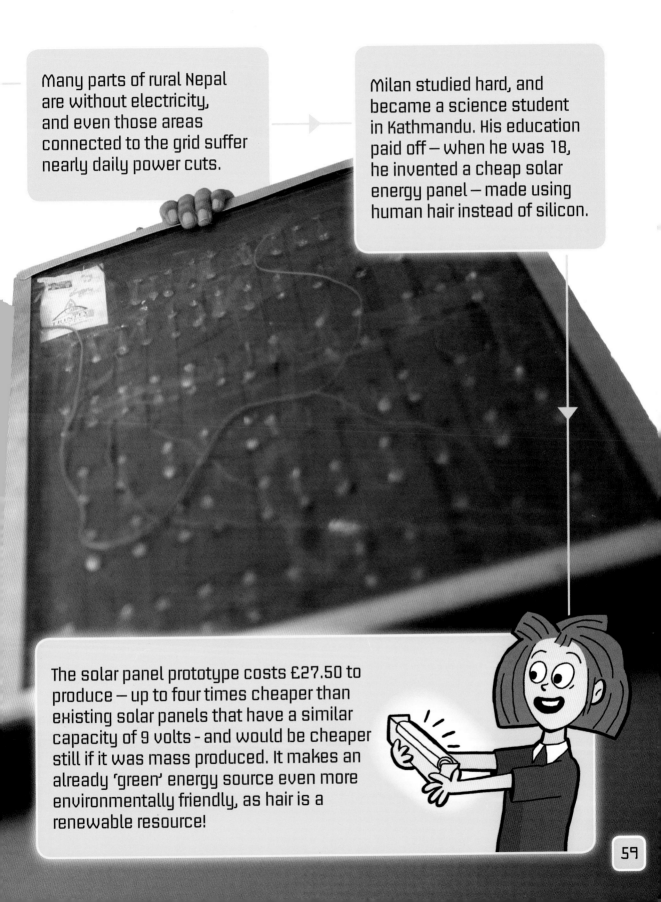

Many parts of rural Nepal are without electricity, and even those areas connected to the grid suffer nearly daily power cuts.

Milan studied hard, and became a science student in Kathmandu. His education paid off — when he was 18, he invented a cheap solar energy panel — made using human hair instead of silicon.

The solar panel prototype costs £27.50 to produce — up to four times cheaper than existing solar panels that have a similar capacity of 9 volts - and would be cheaper still if it was mass produced. It makes an already 'green' energy source even more environmentally friendly, as hair is a renewable resource!

WRISTWATCH

Watches have been around since the 17th century – but early watches were very different from the wristwatches of today. Carried in the pocket, these watches had mechanical mechanisms powered by springs.

A watch worn in World War I

This changed with the outbreak of World War I, when soldiers needed quick access to the time, and their hands free for weapons.

The first watches were pocket watches, which were held on a chain. In the 1900s, the first wristwatches appeared, but they were only worn by women.

Pocket watches are invented.

Abraham-Louis Breguet creates a watch to fit on the wrist of the Queen of Naples.

Aviator Alberto Santos Dumont (right) has a wristwatch made for him to wear while flying.

Wristwatche for men appear durin World War I

Mechanical watch mechanism

Mechanical watches need to be wound up by hand. Today, most watches are electronic, and contain a tiny vibrating quartz crystal.

The latest smartwatches let you make phone calls and surf the Internet.

Electricity makes the crystal vibrate at a constant speed. These vibrations are used to set the time.

Watches now have other functions including stopwatches, alarms and calendars. Some modern watches can even connect to the Internet and forecast the weather.

1965   1972   2013

NASA astronauts start wearing Omega wristwatches.

The first digital watch goes on sale.

The Pebble and Samsung Galaxy Gear smart watches are launched. They can connect to the Internet and mobile phones.

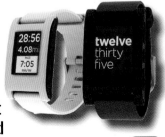

BRANDING

Branding includes the style and appearance of packaging, but also includes the name of a product and the way it is presented. A good name is very important!

Ernö Rubik's name is a key component of the Rubik's Cube brand.

Sometimes products are named using the inventor's name. The Rubik's Cube is named after its inventor, Ernö Rubik. His name has now become famous due to the success of his cube.

Companies often employ advertising agencies to come up with ideas on how to present their products. Advertisements exist to make people want to buy products.

Ferrero Rocher's packaging, advertising and even its name create a feeling of luxury.

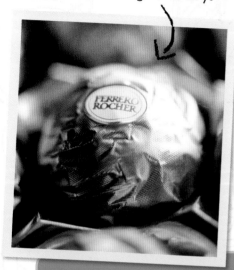

Leaflets and other literature accompanying an item also contribute to branding. The Rubik's Cube came with an instruction manual to help people solve the puzzle – but it was also part of the branding. It used images and text to show that the cube was educational and fun.

Advertisements also help to create a brand, and often emphasize the lifestyle or mood that can be 'bought' along with the product. For example, a type of chocolate might be branded in such a way as to suggest an indulgent, luxurious lifestyle.

Rubik's Cube handbag

» BRAND RUBIK'S

People have liked the Rubik's brand so much, that all sorts of other products have been made. There are Rubik's handbags, furniture made using huge blocks of Rubik's Cubes, Rubik's Cube trainers, Rubik's Cube lamps – and Rubik's Cube cakes!

Rubik's Cube chair

YOUNG INVENTOR'S PORTFOLIO

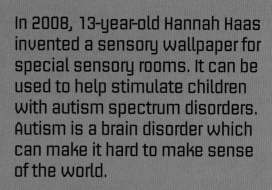

NAME: Hannah Haas

AGE: 13

INVENTION:
Sensory Wallpaper

YEAR: 2008

Hannah's invention was the Grand Prize Winner in the 2008 Bubble Wrap Competition for Young Inventors.

In 2008, 13-year-old Hannah Haas invented a sensory wallpaper for special sensory rooms. It can be used to help stimulate children with autism spectrum disorders. Autism is a brain disorder which can make it hard to make sense of the world.

Hannah wrote an essay to describe her invention and entered it into a competition run by the Bubble Wrap® company. She described how children with autism often find stroking their hands across a textured surface calming.

Bubble Wrap has small air bubbles trapped in a plastic sheet.

POP!

CRACKLE!

Sensory rooms, such as this one, are filled with equipment and decorations that are designed to stimulate mental activity.

Sensory wallpaper ensures that autistic children have the means to calm themselves built into their own environment, making their lives more comfortable.

» OTHER INVENTIONS

Other winners of the annual Bubble Wrap competition include wrist supports to help with carpal tunnel syndrome, special curtains to make refrigerators more efficient, a water-saving device for toilets and a cost-effective cosmetic skin covering for artificial limbs to use in developing countries.

INVENTION TIMELINE

TELEPHONE

The electric telegraph was invented in the 1840s, and the age of the telephone began. Alexander Graham Bell worked on the idea of sending voice messages along telegraph wires. His telephone was patented in 1876 and history was made.

Alexander Graham Bell
1847–1922

In 1946, Bell Labs created a system that allowed users to make calls from their cars.

The history of mobile phones began during the 1940s, when hand-held devices were used by the army to communicate during World War II. It developed further with the use of two-way radios in police cars, taxis and trains. These early phones were very big and bulky, and used lots of power.

1840s	1876	1940s	1946	1973
Electric telegraph invented.	Telephone patented.	Hand-held communication devices used during World War II.	Car phones come onto the market.	First mobile phone call made.

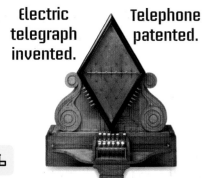

Martin Cooper testing the mobile phone

In 1973, Martin Cooper, a manager at Motorola, made the first ever mobile phone call. He rang Joel Engel, the head of research at Bell Labs. This first mobile phone weighed 1.1 kg and was a huge 13 cm long and 4.45 cm wide! It allowed just 30 minutes of talk and took ten hours to charge.

Mobile phones have come a long way since the early 1970s and are now tiny and reliable. Modern 'smartphones' can connect users to the Internet, like a tiny computer. The latest technology also allows people to enjoy streamed radio and TV programmes on their phones!

1991
Invention of technology that leads to the introduction of WiFi.

2001
3G technology introduced.

2004
Mass-market Voice Over Internet Protocol (VoIP) services allow people to use the Internet to make voice and video calls.

2007
Apple release the iPhone.

2009
4G technology is launched.

» STEP 11
PACKAGING

Packaging helps to protect a product, keeping it safe during transit - the journey from the factory to a shop, and from the shop to the purchaser's house. Packaging also needs to be attractive, so that people notice the product and want to buy it.

Packaging has to protect the product inside. Sometimes a cardboard box is used, as it is sturdy and can cushion the product if it gets dropped or bumped. If cardboard is used, a picture of the product usually features on the outside.

Packaged products will often be stored and transported in crates or on pallets.

This Rubik's Cube packaging includes a protective cardboard case and a window to show people what's inside.

Sometimes clear blister plastic packs are used, as they help to protect a product while also showing people what is inside the package.

Packages need to be a shape that can easily be packed on pallets or in crates. They can then be transported to shops cheaply and efficiently.

Packaging contains information about the product. This information tells people how to use the product safely and how to get the most enjoyment from it.

A code reader identifies the cost and important shipping information.

Good packaging should make a product attractive to buyers.

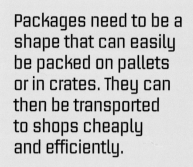

The packaging also contains information about how the product should be handled, where it needs to be sent and how much it costs. This information is usually contained in a special code which can be read using code readers.

RASPBERRY PI

When Eben Upton, a physicist and computer engineer, was teaching at Cambridge University he realized that computers were so expensive that it was difficult for everyone to afford them — and this could make learning difficult.

Eben Upton
1978–present

All the Pi's working parts are visible.

He decided to invent a small, cheap computer that could make computing accessible to all. He created the Raspberry Pi.

Everything has been done to keep the cost of the computer low. It does not come with a plastic case or a DVD drive. As a result, each Raspberry Pi costs just £16.

1820s   1936   1964

Charles Babbage
1791–1871

Charles Babbage designs a difference engine, a mechanical computer.

Konrad Zuse builds the Z1, the first freely programmable computer.

Douglas Engelbart invents the computer mouse.

The Raspberry Pi Foundation was set up as a charity with the aim of making computers affordable for all.

This robot is powered by a Raspberry Pi.

The original model had 256 MB of RAM.

1984

Apple releases the Macintosh computer.

1989

Tim Berners-Lee develops a system that becomes the world wide web.

Tim Berners-Lee 1955–present

2006

Eben Upton devises the Raspberry Pi.

2012

The Raspberry Pi is released.

MARKETING

Marketing is the process of making a product look attractive to customers. Products are marketed through advertising on the television or radio, at the cinema, in newspapers and magazines, online and as billboards. Advertising is everywhere!

Marketing a product means persuading people to buy it. This is often achieved by suggesting that the product will make a person's life better – more fun, for example. Advertisements of the Rubik's Cube show people having a good time.

Eye-catching displays in shops help to market products, because they make people notice them. Advertisers use special stands and settings to make shop and window displays.

Special versions of the Rubik's Cube, like this leather and nickel-trimmed one, create extra publicity.

The world's smallest Rubik's Cube also generates interest.

Images help advertisements to be bright and interesting. Photographers and graphic designers work hard to make advertisements as attractive as possible.

Advertising hoardings in London.

Copywriters come up with jingles and slogans to help sell a product. Look out for examples around you. Musicians write catchy music and songs to help make the advertisement noticeable, so that people remember it.

» CUBIST ART

The Cube Works Studio from Canada re-create works of art using Rubik's Cubes. The artists twist the cubes to form patterns and the cubes are then put together to replicate famous works of art and completely new pieces, including *The Last Supper* by Leonardo da Vinci (below).

Created in 2009, this artwork was 2.59 metres high and 5.18 metres wide and made up of 4050 cubes.

COMPETITIONS AND CLUBS

There are lots of competitions and clubs for young inventors around the world. It's a good way to make you think hard about your ideas and planning and because you have a deadline, it really focuses the mind. It's also a great way to make friends with other inventors! Many science museums and lots of large companies run competitions — look on the Internet and find one that suits you. Good luck!

You might also like to explore some websites for inventors — or join a club. Have a look at these useful sites:

Speed cubers get some practice in at the 2013 Rubik's Cube Championships in Las Vegas, USA.

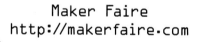

Maker Faire
http://makerfaire.com

Let's Get Inventin'
http://www.younginventors.tv

Academy of Applied Science
http://www.aas-world.org

Science Museum, London
http://www.sciencemuseum.org.uk

Liberty Centre, New York
http://lsc.org

A Canadian competitor attempts to solve the puzzle blindfolded.

Arranging competitions is a great way to promote and market your invention. For example, there are competitions where people try to solve the Rubik's Cube as quickly as possible, with some even using their feet or wearing a blindfold!

Too easy to solve the puzzle with your hands? Try doing it with your feet!

These competitions are a great way of gathering people together in one room. You can use these events to get publicity and to gain exposure in newspapers as well as on the radio and television.

SUMMARY

So, invention is a process. From the first idea, there are many stages to go through on the journey to a product that can be used and sold.

Creating and developing your invention is hard work and not something that can be achieved overnight. There are many stages you will have to go through before your idea has been perfected, but there's no better feeling than seeing your creation become a reality.

AIRBUS
CONCEPT PLANE

Think about what you would like to invent, or talk it through with friends, and always keep a record of any ideas you might have — you never know which one might work.

Will you create a world-changing mode of transport, a new way of making things, or an ecological device that can reduce pollution or energy consumption and save the planet?

» LATEST INVENTIONS

3D printers can produce items such as these shoes quickly and cheaply.

These artificial trees could draw carbon dioxide from the atmosphere and cut pollution.

The latest designs and materials will produce planes that can fly further and more economically.

F-EIAI

You've read about inventors both young and old who have had an impact on the way we run our lives. Now it's your turn. You might not get it right first time, and it will be hard work, but one thing is certain — inventing is exciting!

"Genius is 1 per cent inspiration and 99 per cent perspiration."
Thomas Edison

GLOSSARY

ALGAE
A group of living organisms that produce the energy they need to live and survive from sunlight, but do not have the structures found in plants, such as leaves and roots.

BRAINSTORMING
A way of thinking creatively, either alone or in a group, to come up with a solution to a problem. Inventors use brainstorming to come up with a range of ideas that can be used to develop an invention.

BRANDING
An image or idea used to sell a product. Branding can include packaging and the colours and images used for advertising, as well as the product's name.

BRIEF
A set of instructions that clearly tells someone how you want an object to look and perform.

DESIGN
A design is a detailed plan for something. It helps inventors to work out how a product can be made.

EMBOSS
To push or raise something so that it sits above the surrounding area.

EVALUATION
After an invention has been tested, it needs to be evaluated — that means working out if the product works properly and does the things that it was intended to do when it was designed. It also makes sure that the product is safe to use and will not harm anyone.

EVAPORATION
The process of changing from a liquid into a gas. Water evaporates to form water vapour. Evaporation causes the body of liquid to cool slightly, until it is a similar temperature to its surroundings.

INTELLECTUAL PROPERTY

An idea — such as a plan for an invention — can be intellectual property. It can be stolen like any other property, so it needs to be protected by law. Patents can be registered to protect intellectual property from being copied.

LED

Short for Light-Emitting Diode, these are special lights that emit more light per watt than normal light bulbs. They are used in all sorts of devices, from traffic signals to bicycle lights.

MARKETING

Marketing means a plan for advertising and selling things. Many businesses have marketing plans to help them predict how well a product will sell, and how many units need to be produced.

MASS PRODUCTION

Making things in large numbers is known as mass production. This is usually done in a factory, using machinery. The production costs are reduced dramatically because the objects are made in large numbers.

MODIFICATION

Modification means changing or adapting things. Inventions are often modified after they have been tested, to make improvements.

PATENT

A patent is a legal document that protects an idea or invention. Inventors apply for patents so that other people cannot use, produce or sell things that were not their own original idea.

PROTOTYPE

A prototype is a working model of an invention. It is created to make sure an idea works, and to iron out any problems before it goes into production. Prototypes are sometimes used during the process of applying for a patent, to prove that an invention belongs to a particular inventor.

INDEX